SCHOLASTIC
ENGLISH SKILLS

Comprehension
Workbook

Ages 9–10

Comprehension

Scholastic Education, an imprint of Scholastic Ltd
Book End, Range Road, Witney, Oxfordshire, OX29 0YD
Registered office: Westfield Road, Southam,
Warwickshire CV47 0RA
www.scholastic.co.uk

© 2016, Scholastic Ltd

456789 89012345

British Library Cataloguing-in-Publication Data
A catalogue record for this book is available from the British Library.

ISBN 978-1407-14181-7

Printed in Malaysia

Acknowledgements

The publishers gratefully acknowledge permission to reproduce the following copyright material: **Andersen Press Ltd** for the use of text and an illustration from *The Steadfast Tin Soldier* by Naomi Lewis. Text © 1986, Naomi Lewis. Illustration © 1991, P.J. Lynch. (1991, Andersen Press Ltd). **Cambridge University Press** for the use of an extract from *New Horizons: The life of a car*. © 1994, Cambridge University Press. (1994, Cambridge University Press). **David Higham Associates** for the use of the cover and extracts from *The Brilliant World of Tom Gates* by Liz Pichon. © 2011, Liz Pichon. (2011, Scholastic Children's Books); text from *The Lion Who Stole My Arm* by Nicola Davies. Text © 2013, Nicola Davies. (2013, Walker Books Ltd). **Michael Foreman** for the use of text and illustrations from *War Game* by Michael Foreman. Text and illustrations © 1993, Michael Foreman. (2006, Pavilion Children's Books). **John Foster** for the use of the poem 'The Smugglers' from the collection *Four O'Clock Friday* by John Foster. Text © 1991, John Foster.(1991, Oxford University Press). **Frances Lincoln Children's Books** for the use of text and illustrations from *Azzi In Between* by Sarah Garland. Text and illustrations © 2012, Sarah Garland. (2012, Frances Lincoln Children's Books); text and illustrations from *Stanley Bagshaw and the Twenty Two Ton Whale* by Bob Wilson. Text and illustrations © 2005, Bob Wilson. (2005, Barn Owl Books). **Macmillan Children's Books** for the use of text and illustrations from *Tony Robinson's Weird World of Wonders: Pets* by Tony Robinson. Text © 2014, Sir Tony Robinson. Illustrations © 2014, Del Thorpe. (2014, Macmillan Children's Books); text

and an illustration from *Goth Girl and the Ghost of a Mouse* by Chris Riddell. © 2013, Chris Riddell. (2013, Macmillan Children's Books). **Oxford University Press** for the use of an illustration by Debbie Cook for 'The Smugglers' in *Four O'Clock Friday* by John Foster. Illustration © 1991, Debbie Cook. (1991, Oxford University Press). **Random House Group Ltd** for the use of text and an illustration from *Blitzed* by Robert Swindells. Text © 2002, Robert Swindells. Illustrations © 2002, Robin Lawrie. (2002, Doubleday); text and illustrations from *UG* by Raymond Briggs. Text and illustration © 2001, Raymond Briggs. (2001, Jonathan Cape). **Scholastic Children's Books** for the use of text and illustrations from *The Horrible Science of Everything* by Nick Arnold and Tony De Saulles. Text © 2005, Nick Arnold. Illustration © 2005, Tony De Saulles. (2005, Scholastic Ltd); text and an illustration from *Horrible Geography of the World* by Anita Ganeri. Text © 2007, Anita Ganeri. Illustration © 2007 Mike Phillips. (2007, Scholastic Ltd). **Usborne Publishing** for the use of text and illustration from *Beginners: Vikings* by Stephanie Turnbull. © 2006, Usborne Publishing Ltd. (2006, Usborne Publishing Ltd); text and illustrations from *50 Science Things to Make and Do.* © 2008, 2005 Usborne Publishing Ltd. (2008, Usborne Publishing Ltd). **Walker Books Ltd** for the use of text and illustrations from *Sir Gawain and the Loathly Lady* by Selina Hastings, illustrated by Juan Wijngaard. Text © 1985, Selina Hastings. Illustrations © 1985, Juan Wijngaard. (1985, Walker Books Ltd); text and an illustration from *Ronny Rock Starring in Monster Cake Meltdown* by Merryn Threadgould, illustrated by Bruce Ingman. Text © 2011 Merryn Threadgould. Illustrations © 2011, Bruce Ingman. (2011, Walker Books Ltd); text and illustrations from *Night Sky Dragons* by Mal Peet and Elspeth Graham, illustrated by Patrick Benson. Text © 2014, Mal Peet and Elspeth Graham. Illustrations © 2014, Patrick Benson. (2014, Walker Books Ltd); text and an illustration from *Castle Diary* by Richard Platt, illustrated by Chris Riddell. Text © 1999, Richard Platt. Illustrations © 1999, Chris Riddell. (1999, Walker Books Ltd); text and an illustration from *Mysterious Traveller* by Mal Peet and Elspeth Graham, illustrated by P.J. Lynch. Text © 2013, Mal Peet and Elspeth Graham. Illustrations © 2013, P.J. Lynch. (2013, Walker Books Ltd); text and illustrations from *Painting out the Stars* by Mal Peet and Elspeth Graham. Text © 2011, Mal Peet and Elspeth Graham. Illustrations © 2011, Michael Foreman. (2011, Walker Books Ltd); text and illustrations from *Bravo, Mr William Shakespeare!* by Marcia Williams. Text and illustrations © 2000, Marcia Williams. (2000, Walker Books Ltd). **Wildlife Watch**, The Wildlife Trusts for the use of activity sheets from www.wildlifewatch.org.uk. © 2015, Royal Society of Wildlife Trusts. Illustrations © 2015, Corinne Welch.

Every effort has been made to trace copyright holders for the works reproduced in this book, and the publishers apologise for any inadvertent omissions.

Images

Page 50, Victorian children at work. © Ann Ronan Picture Library/HIP/ TopFoto

Author Donna Thomson
Editorial Rachel Morgan, Anna Hall, Kate Soar, Margaret Eaton
Consultants Hilarie Medler, Libby Allman

Cover and Series Design Neil Salt and Nicolle Thomas
Layout K & S Design
Illustration Gemma Hastilow-Smith
Cover Illustration Eddie Rego

Contents

How to use this book

- *Scholastic English Skills Workbooks* help your child to practise and improve their skills in English.

- The content is divided into chapters that relate to different skills. The final 'Review' chapter contains a mix of questions that bring together all of these skills. These questions increase in difficulty as the chapter progresses.

- Keep the working time short and come back to an activity if your child finds it too difficult. Ask your child to note any areas of difficulty. Don't worry if your child does not 'get' a concept first time, as children learn at different rates and content is likely to be covered at different times throughout the school year.

- Find out more information about comprehension skills and check your child's answers at www.scholastic.co.uk/ses/comprehension.

- Give lots of encouragement, complete the 'How did you do' for each activity and the progress chart as your child finishes each chapter.

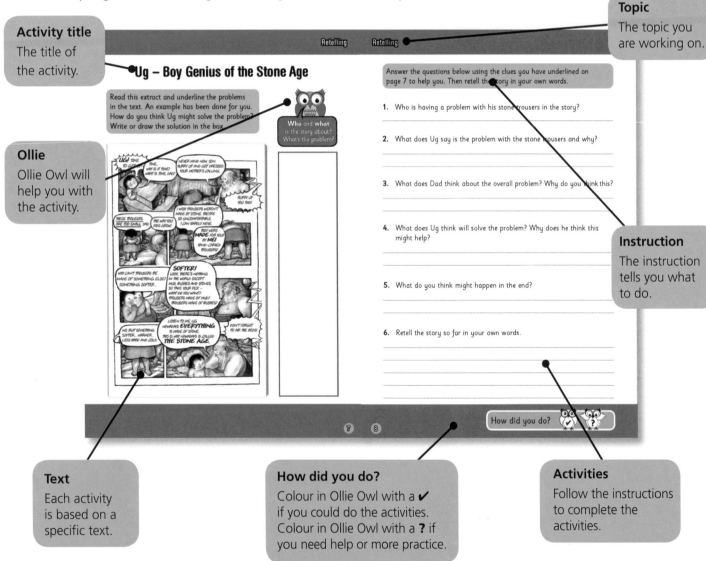

Activity title
The title of the activity.

Ollie
Ollie Owl will help you with the activity.

Topic
The topic you are working on.

Instruction
The instruction tells you what to do.

Text
Each activity is based on a specific text.

How did you do?
Colour in Ollie Owl with a ✔ if you could do the activities. Colour in Ollie Owl with a ? if you need help or more practice.

Activities
Follow the instructions to complete the activities.

If you need help, ask an adult!

Sir Gawain and the Loathly Lady

> **Who** is in the story? **What** are they doing?
> **Where** are they?

Read the beginning of the story *Sir Gawain and the Loathly Lady*. Highlight the 'who', 'what' and 'where' information in different coloured pens. Then retell the beginning of this story in your own words.

KING ARTHUR and his court had moved to the castle of Carlisle for Christmas. Every evening there was feasting and dancing, while by day the King and his knights rode out into the Inglewood to hunt. One morning the King, galloping fast in pursuit of a young stag, found himself separated from his companions, his quarry having outrun the hounds and disappeared. Reining in his horse, he saw that he was in an unfamiliar part of the forest, on the edge of a black and brackish pond surrounded by pine trees whose dark foliage obscured the light of the day. Suddenly Arthur noticed in the shadows on the other side of the pond a man on horseback, watching him. The man was covered from head to foot in black armour, and he sat motionless on a charger which was itself as black as midnight.

6

Once there was _____

_____

_____

_____

Read the text on page 5 again and answer the questions below. Then ask and answer your own question about the story.

The answers are right there in the pictures and text.

1. What is this story about?

_____

_____

2. Who went with King Arthur to Carlisle Castle for Christmas?

_____

3. What kind of activities were available to the King and his court over Christmas?

_____

_____

4. Where did King Arthur and his knights go hunting?

_____

5. What happened when King Arthur went in pursuit of a young stag one morning?

_____

_____

Your question: _____

_____

Your answer: _____

_____

Ug – Boy Genius of the Stone Age

Read this extract and underline the problems in the text. An example has been done for you. How do you think Ug might solve the problem? Write or draw the solution in the box.

Who and **what** is the story about? What's the problem?

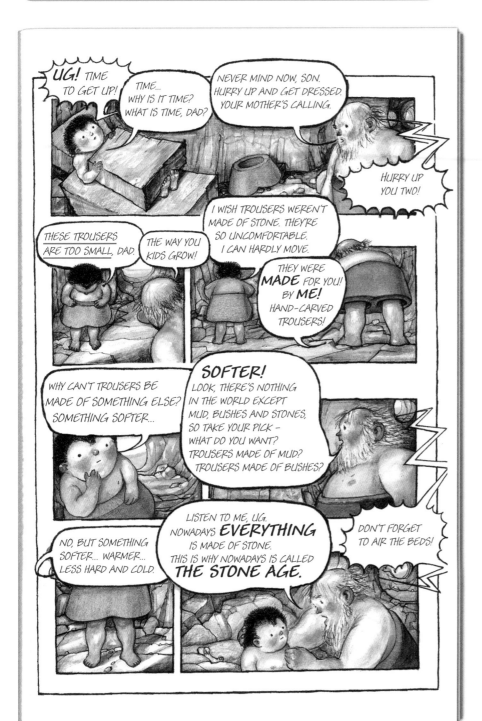

Answer the questions below using the clues you have underlined on page 7 to help you. Then retell the story in your own words.

1. Who is having a problem with his stone trousers in the story?

_____

2. What does Ug say is the problem with the stone trousers and why?

_____

_____

3. What does Dad think about the overall problem? Why do you think this?

_____

_____

4. What does Ug think will solve the problem? Why does he think this might help?

_____

_____

5. What do you think might happen in the end?

_____

_____

6. Retell the story so far in your own words.

_____

_____

_____

_____

_____

How did you do?

How to make a paper compass

Read the instructions below that tell you how to make a paper compass.

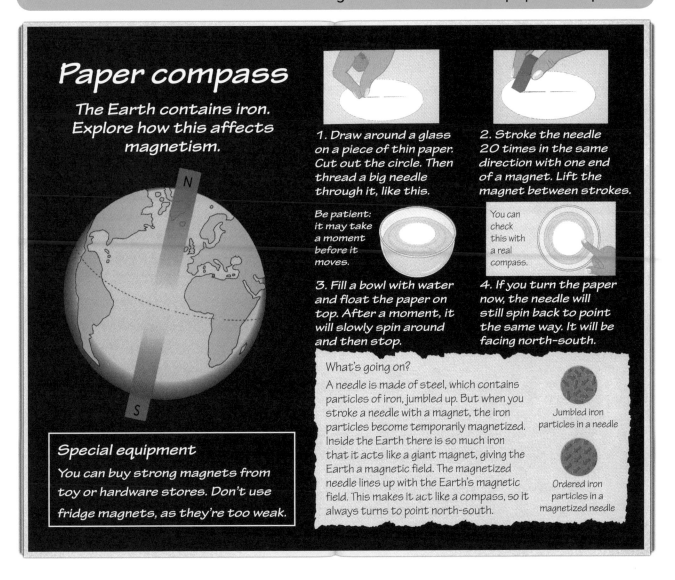

Paper compass

The Earth contains iron. Explore how this affects magnetism.

1. Draw around a glass on a piece of thin paper. Cut out the circle. Then thread a big needle through it, like this.

Be patient: it may take a moment before it moves.

2. Stroke the needle 20 times in the same direction with one end of a magnet. Lift the magnet between strokes.

You can check this with a real compass.

3. Fill a bowl with water and float the paper on top. After a moment, it will slowly spin around and then stop.

4. If you turn the paper now, the needle will still spin back to point the same way. It will be facing north-south.

What's going on?

A needle is made of steel, which contains particles of iron, jumbled up. But when you stroke a needle with a magnet, the iron particles become temporarily magnetized. Inside the Earth there is so much iron that it acts like a giant magnet, giving the Earth a magnetic field. The magnetized needle lines up with the Earth's magnetic field. This makes it act like a compass, so it always turns to point north-south.

Jumbled iron particles in a needle

Ordered iron particles in a magnetized needle

Special equipment

You can buy strong magnets from toy or hardware stores. Don't use fridge magnets, as they're too weak.

List the items you need to make a paper compass below.

1. _____   4. _____   7. _____

2. _____   5. _____   8. _____

3. _____   6. _____

Retell the instructions in your own words and answer the questions below. Then ask and answer your own question about the instructions.

First: _____

_____

Then: _____

_____

Next: _____

_____

Finally: _____

_____

1. What do the instructions tell you to do with a magnet? Explain why you need to do this for the experiment to work.

_____

_____

_____

_____

2. How can you check that the experiment has worked?

_____

_____

Your question: _____

_____

Your answer: _____

_____

How did you do?

Azzi In Between

Read this page from the story *Azzi In Between*.

Who is this story about? What is the problem? How is the problem resolved?

'I was only six when we left our country' said Sabeen...

Sabeen told Azzi the story of her journey.

"I walked with my family through the forest,

and across rivers,

and over mountains,

until we came to a camp.

We stayed at the camp for many years.

Then I was allowed to leave.

But my family had to stay behind, and that was the worst thing.

One day they will join me," said Sabeen. "And one day I think that you will see your Grandma again."

Look carefully at the pictures on page 11 and read the text again. Write the beginning, middle and end of Sabeen's story in your own words.

Beginning: The story is about... (Who? What? Where?)

Middle: The problem is...

End: I think what happens in the end is...

How did you do?

Goth Girl and the Ghost of a Mouse

Read this extract from *Goth Girl and the Ghost of a Mouse*. Use different coloured pens to highlight the 'who', 'what' and 'where' information in the text. Then put the information in the correct columns in the chart below. An example has been done for you.

Being so old and so big, Ghastly-Gorm Hall was home to quite a few ghosts. There was the white nun who sometimes appeared in the long gallery on moonlit nights, the black monk who occasionally haunted the short gallery and the beige curate who slid down the banisters of the grand staircase on the first Tuesday of each month. They usually mumbled, wailed softy or, in the case of the curate, sang in a high-pitched lisping voice, but they never actually *said* anything, unlike this mouse.

'Have you been a ghost for long?' Ada asked, putting the candle down and sitting cross-legged on the carpet.

'I don't think so,' said the ghost of a mouse. 'You see, the last thing I remember was scuttling along the corridor of a dusty, cobwebby part of the house I'd never been in before.' The mouse shimmered palely in the candlelight.

Who	What (doing)	Where
The white nun	sometimes appeared	in the long gallery

Read the text on page 13 again and answer the questions below. Then ask and answer your own 'who', 'what' and 'where' questions, using the information in the table on page 13.

The **literal** answers are right there in the text.

1. What happened in the long gallery at Ghastly-Gorm Hall some nights?

_____

2. Who never said anything, but mumbled, wailed or sang in a high-pitched lisping voice?

_____

3. Where had the mouse never been to before?

_____

Your 'who' question: _____

Your answer: _____

_____

Your 'what' question: _____

Your answer: _____

_____

Your 'where' question: _____

Your answer: _____

_____

How did you do?

Tony Robinson's Weird World of Wonders

Read this extract from *Tony Robinson's Weird World of Wonders*. Then go through it again and highlight the characters, actions and places in different coloured pens.

Who and **what** is the text about?

When Edward VII died, Caesar was heartbroken and spent days outside his master's bedroom door, whining and refusing to eat. At the King's funeral he was given the honour of walking behind the coffin.

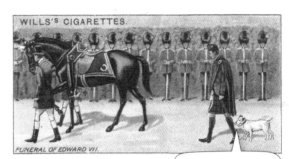

WILLS'S CIGARETTES.

FUNERAL OF EDWARD VII.

Where's the coffin gone? Where's it gone!

But it wasn't just dogs that were popular in royal circles.

Charles XII of Sweden had a favourite cat which used to lie on his desk and sleep on his papers. Rather than disturb him, the King wrote around the cat, leaving a blank cat-shape on his letters!

Queen Elizabeth of Bohemia was famous for keeping pet monkeys. People said she liked them better than her own children.

Maybe I did!

Ferdinand IV of Naples filled the rooms of his palace with chickens, pigeons, ducks, geese, canaries, cats and dogs. He also had cages full of mice, which he'd sometimes let out just for the fun of it.

Use the information you have underlined on page 15 to answer these questions. Then ask and answer your own literal questions.

The answers to **literal** questions are right there in the text.

1. Who was heartbroken when King Edward VII died?

_____

2. What did the King's dog do for days after his master died?

_____

_____

3. Where was Caesar during the King's funeral?

_____

Your literal question: _____

Answer: Ferdinand IV filled his palace with animals in Naples.

Your literal question: _____

Your answer: _____

_____

Your literal question: _____

Your answer: _____

_____

How did you do?

Monster Cake Meltdown

Answers to **literal** questions are right there in the text and pictures.

Read the text and picture information from *Monster Cake Meltdown*. Then read the questions on page 18 and underline the words that are the same in the questions and text. An example has been done for you.

Lots of children had their birthday <u>parties</u> on Saturdays. So, <u>Friday afternoons</u> were spent <u>making birthday cakes</u> and Ronny loved to help.

He found Mr Rock standing at a table with a pile of plain cake on one side and a pile of sweets and icing on the other.

"Ah, Captain Rock," said his dad. "Your flight's bang on schedule. Read these birthday letters out to me and help me work my magic." He handed Ronny a bunch of cake request letters and flourished his icing knife like a magician's wand. Ronny ate the last bit of doughnut and read the first request.

Search for key words that are the same in the question and in the text. Remember the answer to the question will be nearby.

Write your answers below using the matching information that you have underlined in the questions and text. Then ask and answer your own literal questions.

1. Who spent <u>Friday afternoons helping</u> to <u>make birthday cakes</u> for <u>parties</u>?

    _____

2. Where was his dad standing when Ronny found him?

    _____

3. What did his dad call him before he said, 'Your flight's bang on schedule'?

    _____

4. Who flourished his knife like a magician's wand?

    _____

Your literal question: _____

Your answer: _____

_____

Your literal question: _____

Your answer: _____

_____

How did you do?

The Brilliant World of Tom Gates

Skim left to right. **Scan** up and down to locate key words.

Read this extract from *The Brilliant World of Tom Gates*.

The tent was tricky to put up, but we did the best we could.

It was a bit late to eat. Dad said, "I'll cook a big breakfast in the morning." But my stomach kept 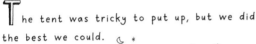 and I couldn't get to sleep. Then I remembered the secret stash of biscuits in my bag. So I grabbed them and ate them all! Crumbs got everywhere and it was very uncomfortable in my sleeping bag. Even though we had a "family tent" with separate rooms, Delia could hear me shifting around and fidgeting. It was really annoying her. BRILLIANT! So I did it some more. But at the same time I could also hear Mum and Dad ...

(20)

 and that was keeping me awake too. The noise was awful. It seemed to be getting louder and LOUDER. It was almost like thunder, deep and rumbly. Then I realized it sounded like thunder ... because it was thunder. Which was getting closer. There was lightning, too, and really heavy rain that was right above our tent. The storm was HUGE and it didn't take long for the tent to blow away. (AGH!) (HELP!)

Everyone had to run to the car for cover. The storm lasted all night long and everything we had got wet and muddy. Dad had pitched the tent RIGHT NEXT TO A STREAM! Which flooded and all our stuff got soaked.
Nobody slept at all. It was miserable.

(21)

Skim and scan the text to find the following key words in the story.
Underline each word in the text as you find it. One has been done for you.

stream   car   stomach   snoring   crumbs
cook   wet   muddy   nobody   shifting   storm

Skim and scan the text on page 19 for the words in bold in the following questions. Use these and the words you have underlined in the text to answer the questions about Tom's camping trip with his family. Then ask and answer your own literal question using a key word from the text.

1. Who said, 'I'll cook a big **breakfast** in the morning'?

_____

2. What was Tom doing that Delia found really **annoying**?

_____

3. Where was the tent **pitched**?

_____

4. List three of the things keeping Tom **awake** so he couldn't get to **sleep**?

a. _____

b. _____

c. _____

5. What did the family do when the **tent** blew **away**?

_____

6. What happened to **everything** in the storm?

_____

Your literal question: _____

Your answer: _____

_____

How did you do?

The life of a car

> Think about the consequences of the designers' actions.

Read this information about interior car design. Highlight clues that suggest what might happen to drivers or their passengers if these safety and comfort features are not considered.

The car's trim

The engine makes a car go, but the car would not be useable and comfortable to drive without its 'trim'. This word describes things such as the seats, windows, electrical equipment, and the panelling and lining inside the car.

1 Designers make drawings of the dashboard, controls and seats.

2 They base their measurements on the average height of a person...

3 ...how far he or she can comfortably stretch arms and legs...

4 ...and 'eye lines'. This means how far a person can see without moving his or her head.

5 The driver's view of instruments and gauges must not be blocked by parts of the car such as the steering column.

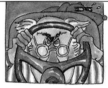

Designing seats and controls

It is very important that the driver is comfortable and can reach all the controls easily. Badly designed seats lead to backache and stiffness. It is dangerous if the driver's attention is distracted by having to look down or reach for a control.

6 The seats have to be adjustable. They slide forwards or backwards to suit people of different heights.

7 The back can be adjusted so that the driver can sit upright...

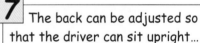

8 ...or lean back.

9 The backs of the seats are shaped to support the driver's and passengers' backs properly.

Use the information you have highlighted to list three points that are important when designing seats and controls. Predict how each might affect drivers' or passengers' safety or comfort.

This happened (effect) because of that (cause).

1. _____

_____

2. _____

_____

3. _____

_____

Choose one point from your list. Imagine that it has been designed badly. Predict how the safety or comfort of the driver or passengers might be affected. Draw or write how the design fault causes a problem, what effect this has on the driver/passengers and what the consequences might be for them after that.

1. The design fault (the cause)

2. What happens (immediate effect)

3. The consequences (longer-term effect)

How did you do?

Azzi In Between

Read this page and circle clues in the pictures and text that suggest what might have happened before and what might happen next to this family. Then answer the questions on page 24.

Use your knowledge about the world and the clues on the page to make your predictions.

Hold tight, sweetheart!

On the jetty, the people were shoving and pushing, trying to reach the boat, trying to escape from the dangers of the war.
Father and Mother pushed too, with all their strength.

They struggled down a ladder to the boat and jumped on board.
"That's it! No more!" cried the boatman, as he cast off the mooring rope.
He revved up the engine, the boat turned, and they were out in the open sea.

1. What do you predict is the theme of the story? Tick the correct box.

   ☐ courage   ☐ joy   ☐ hope

   Explain why you think this. _____

   _____

2. Predict what you think might have happened before these scenes. Why do you think this?

   _____

   _____

   _____

3. Why do you think the family has chosen to escape by boat? Explain why you think this.

   _____

   _____

   _____

4. What do you predict will happen to the people who are left behind? Why do you think this?

   _____

   _____

   _____

5. Describe what you think might happen next to the family. Explain why you think this.

   _____

   _____

   _____

How did you do?

Book covers

Look carefully at the book cover below. Circle clues in the text and design that suggest what the book might be about. Think about the style of font, subject matter, illustrations and type of book.

Look for clues in the cover text and picture.

Use the clues on the cover to help you answer the questions below. Then ask and answer your own prediction question about the book.

1. From the clues in the title and cover design, what type of book do you think this is? Why do you say this?

    _____

    _____

    _____

2. From the information on the cover, do you predict that the stories inside might be humorous? Why do you think this?

    _____

    _____

    _____

3. What do you predict Tom Gates' hobbies might be, from the clues on the cover? Give your reasons.

    _____

    _____

    _____

    _____

Your prediction question: _____

_____

Your answer: _____

_____

_____

How did you do?

First World War poster

Read the information below and look carefully at the poster. Underline the clues in the text and circle the picture clues to help you predict the full meaning of this wartime poster.

Link the clues and your knowledge about the First World War to predict the poster message.

During the First World War the Government needed to recruit lots of soldiers and wanted people to work together to save resources. So what the public thought about the First World War really mattered. The Government tried hard to persuade people to think in a certain way and to feel proud of themselves and their country. This is called propaganda.

Posters with bold images and words were printed to strengthen the propaganda message. For example, this poster is urging the public to eat less bread to spare merchant ships from attack on their way back to Britain with food supplies from faraway countries such as America. By 1917 four hundred ships each month were being destroyed by the 'unseen' enemy in the sea beneath them.

Use the clues on page 27 to help you answer the questions below. Then ask and answer your own prediction question about the poster.

1. Why do you think that eating less bread would 'save the wheat' as the poster suggests?

_____

_____

2. Why do you think Britain had to import wheat from other countries like America during the war?

_____

_____

_____

_____

3. Why do you think so many merchant ships were sunk before they were able to return to Britain with food supplies?

_____

_____

4. Why do you think 'saving the wheat' would 'help the fleet'?

_____

_____

Your prediction question: _____

_____

Your answer: _____

_____

How did you do?

Horrible Geography of the World

What literal questions could you ask using this information?

Read this page from *Horrible Geography of the World* about an earthquake. Highlight the 'who', 'what' and 'where' information in different coloured pens. Then circle the inference clues on the page that help you think more deeply about what is happening. One has been done for you.

The good news is, seismologists can give very general warnings about where a quake might strike. The bad news is, they only know a quake's on the way when it's actually happening. To make matters worse, some quakes strike without any warning at all. Like the one that hit Tangshan, China, in 1976. Here's how the Daily Globe might have reported from the scene of the disaster.

DAILY 🌐 GLOBE

TANGSHAN, CHINA, 29 July 1976

The surviving residents of this shattered city are still reeling from the shock after yesterday's devastating earthquake.

Measuring a massive 8.3 on the Richter scale, shell-shocked experts are already claiming the quake was the deadliest of modern times.

At 3.43 am, local time, a huge tremor struck without warning. In seconds, it reduced this thriving industrial city to a pile of rubble. Numbers are still coming in, but it is estimated that more than 300,000 people have died. Thousands more lie injured or buried beneath the collapsed buildings. Rescue teams have already begun a frantic search for survivors. Thousands of people have been left homeless. With winter coming, their future looks very bleak indeed.

Use the information in the text on page 29 to help you answer the questions below. Tick the PC Page box next to the literal questions and tick the Text Detective box next to the inference questions.

Literal answers are right there in the picture and text. **Inference** answers link to clues in the text.

Question	PC Page	Text Detective
1. Where did the deadliest quake of modern times happen?	❑	❑
2. Why did experts claim that this earthquake was the deadliest in modern times?	❑	❑
3. Was the city a successful industrial centre before it was destroyed by the quake? How do you know this?	❑	❑
4. Was the quake over quickly? Explain how you know this.	❑	❑
5. What did rescue teams do immediately after the quake?	❑	❑

How did you do?

Night Sky Dragons

Read this page from *Night Sky Dragons*. Circle the clues in the words and picture that suggest what is happening in the story. Then use the clues to help you answer the questions on page 32.

Think about **how you know** what is happening in the text.

The boy clomped across the yard in his heavy winter boots, scattering the fluffed-up and sulky chickens. He stomped up the steps to the walkway that ran inside the high walls of the han. He climbed the ladder (that rose to the rampart) above the huge wood and iron gates and squinted out at the world. His face was small under the felt cap and above the collar of his goatskin coat. It looked like a fingertip poking through a hole in a glove.

The watchmen smiled when they greeted him. "Ho, Yazul! You're up early. You expecting someone?"

The low red sun spilled light into the valley and painted purple shadows on the endless, snow-smothered mountains that surrounded it.

"No," Yazul said. "I thought perhaps spring might have come."

The taller watchman shook his head. "No, not yet, Yazul. It's late this year. But soon. I can almost smell it."

Highlight the **clue words** in the questions before you look for answers in the text and pictures.

Use the text and picture on page 31 to help you answer these questions. Then ask and answer your own inference question.

1. Is this story <u>set in modern-day Britain</u>? How do you know this?

_____

_____

_____

_____

2. Explain how you know that the men in the picture are lookouts.

_____

_____

_____

3. Were the men pleased to see Yazul? How do you know this?

_____

_____

4. Was it unusual for Yazul to join the men so early in the day? Explain how you know this.

_____

_____

Your inference question: _____

_____

Your answer: _____

_____

How did you do?

Collecting honey –
Trekking in the Congo Rainforest

Read the text and circle the clues that explain why collecting honey is dangerous in the Congo Rainforest.

Mossapoula, Congo Rainforest

The BaAka men who collect honey are amongst the most respected in the village. It is a dangerous process, and many men die. The honey collector climbs the tree by using an axe to cut notches for footholds and wrapping a liana vine around himself and the trunk as a harness. When he reaches the crown of the tree, he leaves the safety of his harness and walks carefully along a narrow branch to the nest. Now the bees start to attack, and he must get to the honey before he is overcome by their stings. He uses a smoking branch to distract the bees, but he still gets stung. After hacking through the branches to the hive, he removes the honeycomb. The BaAka use honey as a sweetener, and they also eat it straight from the comb. It is considered a great delicacy.

The honey collector wraps a liana vine around himself and the trunk as a harness.

Complete the sentence below using the circled clues on page 33 and 'because' to explain why collecting honey is dangerous. The first one has been done for you.

Collecting honey is a dangerous activity in the rainforest...

1. *because many of the BaAka men die doing it.*

2. _____

3. _____

4. _____

5. _____

Use the clues circled on page 33 to help you answer the questions below. Then ask and answer your own inference question about the text.

Underline the key words in the questions before you search for answers in the text.

1. Why are the men who collect honey the most admired in a BaAka village?

_____

2. Do the BaAka men use any equipment when they climb the trees for honey? How do you know?

_____

_____

Your inference question: _____

_____

Your answer: _____

_____

How did you do?

The smugglers

Read the poem below. Circle the clues on the page that suggest **what** the characters are doing, **where** they are and **why**. Write the clues in the box below. Two examples have been done for you.

The smugglers

Through the sea-mist
Two small boats glide,
Slipping ashore
On the evening tide.

A man with a lantern
Flashes a light
To warn those on shore,
'We're coming tonight.'

A messenger hurries
From door to door,
Whispering softly,
'They're coming ashore.'

Down the cliff path
Six shadows glide
To the foot of the cliff
Where they crouch and hide.

They watch and wait,
Not saying a word,
Until the sound
Of the oars is heard.

Then, quickly, they hurry
Across the sand.
The barrels are passed
From hand to hand.

They are stacked in the cave
And hidden away
Till it's safe to move them
Another day.

Then, back to their beds
The shadows glide,
While the boats slip away
On the outgoing tide.

slipping ashore   flashes a light

Answer these questions about the poem using the clues you have gathered and 'because' to explain how you know. Then write your own inference question and answer.

Highlight the key words in the questions before you search for answers in the clues.

1. Are the two boats coming ashore in secret in the poem? How do you know this?

    _____

    _____

    _____

2. Is the man with the lantern signalling from the boat to a 'lookout' on shore? How do you know?

    _____

    _____

    _____

3. Are the 'six shadows' that are watching and waiting, shadows of smugglers or coast guards? Explain how you know that.

    _____

    _____

    _____

    _____

    Your inference question: _____

    _____

    Your answer: _____

    _____

How did you do?

Blitzed

Read this extract from the time-travel story *Blitzed*. To help you clarify what is happening, underline the words that relate to the **past**, **present** and **future** in different coloured pens. Some examples have been done for you.

Look out for changes in tense that indicate a time change in the text.

Sixty-Seven

'Where've you *been*, George Wetherall: we've had the place upside *down* looking for you.'

Where've I been? Now that's what I *call* a question. How do I answer? *Please miss, I've been to nineteen-forty*, or *Please, miss, I've been to London*. Both true, but who's going to believe? Reckon I'd better settle for the dead-safe *Please, miss, I don't know*.

I don't give *any* of these answers. Fact is I'm so mind-blowingly, gob-smackedly glad to be back; so throat-achingly, eye-wateringly happy to see everybody, *including* Eve Eden, that I don't answer at *all*. Instead I fling my arms round Miss Rossiter like Ma grabbing Rags and burst out crying.

She's so embarrassed she doesn't know whether to comfort me or fight me off. 'It's all *right*, Georgie,' she twitters, twisting to get my bubbly nose off her neck. 'You

shouldn't have wandered off like that but it's not the end of the world, for goodness' sake. We shan't be *expelling* you or anything like that.'

Everybody's gawping at us, kids and strangers alike. Some probably think we're part of the exhibit. BOMBED-OUT FAMILY IN EMOTIONAL REUNION. After a bit old Rossiter manages to break free without looking brutally insensitive and we leave the 'blitz' hut. I gather we were all supposed to eat in the NAAFI canteen some time ago, but my disappearance has caused a postponement. As we hurry towards it now, I pluck at the teacher's sleeve.

'Miss, what *day* is this?' Well, I'm confused: I've been gone a fortnight and everybody's still here, rushing towards a two-week-old lunch. Won't it have got a bit *cold* by now? Won't our folks be wondering where the heck we've got to?

She looks at me like I'm some sort of nut. 'It's *Thursday*, George. It's been Thursday all day: it will remain Thursday until midnight, at which time we shall all be tucked up in our beds, unless of course you plan to disappear again – in which case who knows *when* we'll get home?'

So it's like Scrooge. You know: *the spirits have done it all in one night*. I look at my watch. My so-called American watch. As far as I can tell, I ducked under that barrier just over an hour ago. A fortnight in an hour. I can feel a massive traffic-jam inside my skull: stuff to think about. Wonder about. To remember. It's all in there, gridlocked. It'll get sorted, it'll *have* to, only not now. Not yet.

For here's the NAAFI. The Navy, Army and Air Force Institute, I think it means.

Inside I stop giving a stuff what it means, because the place is fat and fragrant with burgers and sausages and hot dogs and chips, and jelly and trifle and death by chocolate. There isn't a watery spud or a thin cabbage stew or a ration book in sight. Nobody's playing Snakes and Ladders in the light from a Tilley lamp, and nobody's dropping bombs.

It'll do for now.

Put the key past, present and future information that you have underlined into the correct columns below. Some examples have been given. Then answer the questions on the next page using this information.

Past (in red pen)	**Present** (in green pen)	**Future** (in blue pen)
London, 1940.	Glad to be back. Happy to see everybody.	Who's going to believe it?

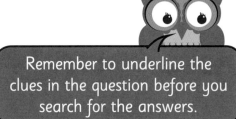

Answer the questions below using the time clues from the text. Then ask and answer your own question about time in the story.

Remember to underline the clues in the question before you search for the answers.

1. What year and place had George travelled back to?

_____

2. Where is the story set in the present day? Explain why you say this.

_____

_____

_____

_____

3. Why is everyone surprised by George's display of emotion when he sees them again?

_____

_____

4. What time delay does George experience between 'wandering off' and returning? How do you know this?

_____

_____

Your clarification question: _____

_____

Your answer: _____

_____

How did you do?

Castle Diary

Read this entry from *Castle Diary*, which is written as if it is the diary of a young page in 1285. The text contains words and phrases from this period in history that may be unfamiliar to you. Circle these words as you come across them.

Search for context clues in the diary to help you clarify the meanings of these words and phrases. Then answer the questions on page 41.

If you come across an unfamiliar word or phrase in the diary, try to use the rest of the sentence to help you clarify its meaning.

January 11th, Thursday

I awoke this morning early and had chance to observe the other pages while they slept. The one who woke next shared some bread with me. He told me his name was Mark and asked me mine. As we ate he pointed at the other sleeping pages, and laughed: "See Toby – Oliver and Humphrey shall have no bread, for they slumber still."

Soon Simon came to take me to the Great Hall, where my Aunt Elizabeth sat by a huge fire. She welcomed me fondly and told me that my uncle attends the King in the west of the country, but will return in a few days.

Then my aunt bade me greet my other cousins, Simon's sisters, Abigail and Beth. Abigail, who is the fairer of face, is younger than I, and her sister is older. When we were introduced Abigail blushed and looked at me from the tail of her eye. "Toby is here to learn the duties of a page," my aunt told them, "but this day I would like you to show him our home." Then, turning to me, she added that on the morrow I would learn what I must do to make myself useful.

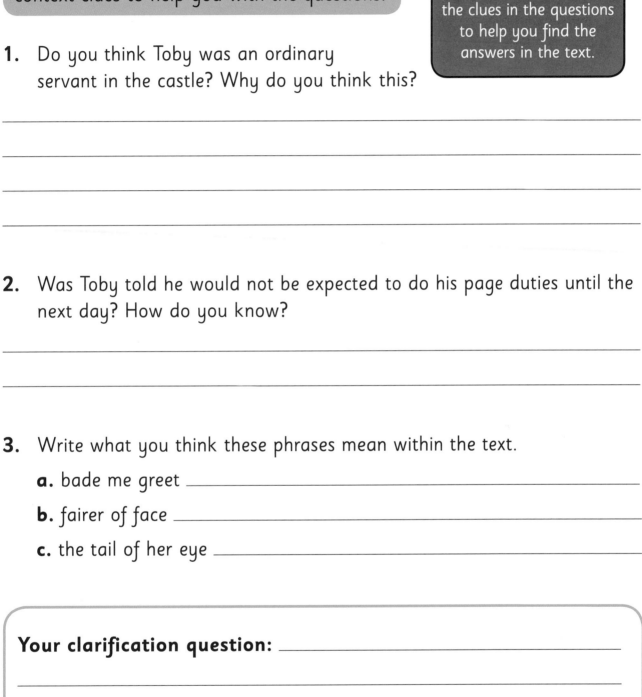

Answer the questions below. Then ask and answer your own question about unfamiliar words from the text. Remember to search for context clues to help you with the questions.

Remember to underline the clues in the questions to help you find the answers in the text.

1. Do you think Toby was an ordinary servant in the castle? Why do you think this?

_____

_____

_____

_____

2. Was Toby told he would not be expected to do his page duties until the next day? How do you know?

_____

_____

3. Write what you think these phrases mean within the text.

    a. bade me greet _____

    b. fairer of face _____

    c. the tail of her eye _____

    Your clarification question: _____

    _____

    Your answer: _____

    _____

    _____

Mysterious Traveller

Read the text below from *Mysterious Traveller* by Mal Peet and Elspeth Graham. Underline the **similes** and circle the **metaphors** in the text. Examples have been done for you. Then answer the questions on page 43 using this information.

Mariama climbed the steep path. It was just a crack in the rock. In places it was only a little wider than her body. When at last she reached the top, she stood wide-eyed and hardly able to breathe.

The mountains stretched before her to the very edge of distance. Some had peaks that were <u>flat-topped and grooved like huge and ancient teeth</u>. Others were bent and twisted like goats' horns, while others were slender and pointed like minarets. And they were all a deep, dark blue, like the scarves of the camel-traders who came from the north. But then, as Mariama watched, the light of (the rising sun touched the tips of the mountains and painted them) a glowing, burning gold.

She cried out aloud because she had never seen anything so beautiful, so magical. And as the sun climbed higher, the golden light slid down the teeth, the horns, the minarets. The blue drained away, and now she saw that dark valleys curled among the mountains like the roots of a tree. And from one of these valleys, not far away, arose a little twist of smoke.

Write the answers to the questions using the words you have underlined and circled in the text. Then ask and answer your own clarification question about the similes or metaphors in the passage.

1. Was Mariama impressed by the scenery when she reached the top of the path? How do you know?

   _____

2. Give an example of how the author combines a metaphor and simile to describe how Mariama views the shape of the valleys in the changing light. Why do you think this description is effective?

   _____

   _____

   _____

   _____

   _____

3. How does the author give the sun and sunlight almost human qualities?

   _____

   _____

4. Are the mountain peaks similar to look at? Explain why you say this.

   _____

   _____

   Your clarification question: _____

   _____

   Your answer: _____

   _____

How did you do?

The Steadfast Tin Soldier

Read this extract from the traditional tale *The Steadfast Tin Soldier*. Skim and scan the text to find synonyms or antonyms for the words in the boxes below. Circle them as you find them and write them on the lines provided.

Synonyms have similar meanings. Antonyms have opposite meanings.

Synonyms

Example:
correct / *proper*

thrown / _____

street children / _____

resolute / _____

heavy rain / _____

THE servant-girl and the little boy went to search in the street, but although they were almost treading on the soldier they somehow failed to see him. If he had called out, "Here I am!" they would have found him easily, but he didn't think it proper behaviour to cry out when he was in uniform.

Now it began to rain; the drops fell fast – it was a drenching shower. When it was over, a pair of urchins passed. "Look!" said one of them. "There's a tin soldier. Let's put him out to sea."

So they made a boat out of newspaper and put the tin soldier in the middle, and set it in the fast-flowing gutter at the edge of the street. Away he sped, and the two boys ran beside him clapping their hands. Goodness, what waves there were in that gutter-stream, what rolling tides! It had been a real downpour. The paper boat tossed up and down, sometimes whirling round and round, until the soldier felt quite giddy. But he remained as steadfast as ever, not moving a muscle, still looking straight in front of him, still shouldering arms.

Antonyms

Example:
with difficulty / *easily*

dry / _____

whispered / _____

behind / _____

lost / _____

Underline the key words in the questions that link to similar or opposite words in the text on page 44. Think about the meanings of the words.

Write the answers to the questions using synonyms and antonyms from the text to help you. Then ask and answer your own clarification question about the passage using a synonym or an antonym.

Example:

Question: Do you think the tin soldier's <u>correct behaviour</u> made him <u>more difficult to find</u>? Explain why you say that.

Answer: Yes, the tin soldier's correct behaviour made him more difficult to find because 'he didn't think it <u>proper behaviour</u> to cry out when he was in uniform' which would have helped them <u>find him</u> more <u>easily</u>.

---

1. Why do you think the paper boat zipped along in the gutter water and was thrown around so much?

    _____

    _____

    _____

2. Was the tin soldier still as upright as ever despite being thrown around constantly in the paper boat? Explain how you know.

    _____

    _____

Your clarification question: _____

_____

Your answer: _____

_____

How did you do?

Night Sky Dragons

Read this extract from *Night Sky Dragons*. How do the words explain the characters' feelings? Look closely at the picture. What does the body language tell you about how they are feeling? Circle any clues you find.

The story of the old ones who had been swallowed up by time. Their troubles and travels, their marriages and great moments had been painted onto the dish. Many hands whose bones were now dust had worked on it. From his earliest childhood, Yazul had sat with his grandmother while her old fingers traced the tales and recited the names. His eyes had grown wider when she pointed to the dragons that appear in the sky when the gods are angry.

The dish was older than memory. It was his grandmother's most valued possession. And now Yazul's foolishness had destroyed it.

His grandmother turned and looked at him. Her eyes were full of tears now, and her voice was broken.

"Yazul, Yazul. What have you done?" He could not speak.

His grandfather appeared, his eyes full of anxiety. When he saw the shards on the ground his face turned to stone. He squatted and studied them.

Yazul made his voice work. "Can you mend it, Grandpa?"

"No," the old man said. "No, I do not think so."

His grandmother turned away from Yazul, then spoke to the sky.

"It is a sign. Our family has come to its end."

"Nonsense," the old man said. "Superstitious nonsense."

"It is a broken dish and nothing more." But he did not look at his grandson.

Answer the questions below. Remember to underline the clues in the questions to help you find the answers in the picture and text. Then ask and answer your own evaluation question about the characters' actions and feelings.

Evaluation questions have no right or wrong answer – as long as you link your ideas to the information in the story.

1. Do you think the dish might have been as important to Yazul as it was to his grandmother? Why do you say that?

_____

_____

_____

2. How do you think Yazul's grandfather felt when he saw the dish in pieces? Explain why he might have reacted this way.

_____

_____

_____

3. Do you think Yazul felt nervous when he asked if his grandfather could mend the dish? Explain why you think that?

_____

_____

_____

Your evaluation question: _____

_____

Your answer: _____

_____

How did you do?

War Game

Read this extract from *War Game* about soldiers living on the front line in the First World War.

Look for the 'who', 'what' and 'where' information right there on the page. Then circle clues that explain what is happening and how the characters are feeling.

Remember to use your literal and inference skills, as well as personal experience to think about the characters' feelings and actions in the story.

The newcomers quickly learned the routine of trench life. An hour before dawn every morning they received the order to 'Stand To'. Half asleep and frozen, the men climbed on to the fire-step, rifles clutched with numb fingers and bayonets fixed.

The half light of dawn and dusk was when an attack was most expected, and both sides had their trenches fully manned at those times. Sometimes nothing happened. Often there was a furious exchange of rifle and machine-gun fire to discourage any attack through the gloom. This was known as 'morning hate'.

After an hour or so the order was given to 'Stand Down'. Only the sentries remained on the fire-step and the rest of the men enjoyed what breakfast they could get among the rats, blood-red slugs and horned beetles that infested the trenches.

Each company going to the Front Line took food for three days, usually bully beef, tins of jam and bone-hard biscuit. Army biscuit had to be smashed with a shovel or bayonet. The pieces were then soaked in water for a couple of days and were sometimes added to soup.

Dugouts were dug into the sides of trenches and roofed with timber or corrugated iron and covered with a minimum of 9 inches of earth and sandbags.

Sometimes the rats would suddenly disappear. Old soldiers thought this to be a sure sign of imminent heavy shelling.

Think about the different question types below and answer the questions. Then ask and answer your own inference and evaluation questions about the story.

1.   What is this story about?

_____

2.   Were attacks in the trenches common during the first light of morning and late evening? How do you know this?

_____

_____

3.   Why do you think the furious exchange of rifle and machine-gun fire at dawn was known as 'morning hate'?

_____

_____

_____

Your inference question: _____

_____

Your answer: _____

_____

Your evaluation question: _____

_____

Your answer: _____

_____

How did you do?

49

Victorian children at work

Look at the picture and read the text about Victorian children in the workplace. For each of the statements in the table below, decide if you think the information is true or false and circle your answer. Underline any clues in the text that help you to decide. One has been done for you.

Life for children in Victorian times was hard and <u>child deaths were common in the workplace</u>. Most children were forced to work extremely long hours for meagre wages. They had no choice because the money was needed to help their families survive. Children were often expected to work 16-hour days in appalling conditions.

Children were useful employees because they were small and could fit into tiny spaces like chimneys and ventilation shafts in mines. They could even crawl under machinery when it was necessary. It was for this reason that children were sent to work almost as soon as they could walk. Children were also much cheaper to employ than adults. This was especially true of the many orphans and street children, who would not be missed if an accident occurred.

Statement	True or false?
1. Victorian workplaces had lots of rules and regulations to ensure that they were safe.	**True / False**
2. Conditions in Victorian workplaces were so terrible that many children refused to work in them.	**True / False**
3. Small boys from the age of 5 were sent up chimneys to brush the soot away.	**True / False**
4. Some factory children worked from 5:00 in the morning until 9:00 at night.	**True / False**
5. Most factory owners preferred to employ adults rather than children because they were cheaper.	**True / False**
6. Orphanage children were hired by employers because they could be replaced easily if accidents occurred.	**True / False**

Use your personal experience, knowledge and evidence from the text to answer the questions below. Then ask and answer your own evaluation question about the information.

Remember, evaluation questions have no right or wrong answer - as long as you link your ideas to the information on the page.

1. Do you think Victorians cared about health and safety? Why do you say that?

_____

_____

_____

2. Do you think the text about Victorian children in the workplace was written simply to inform? Why do you say that?

_____

_____

_____

3. Give an example of the author's attempt to shock the reader. Do you think she is successful? Explain why you think so.

_____

_____

_____

Your evaluation question: _____

_____

Your answer: _____

_____

_____

How did you do?

The Lion Who Stole My Arm

Look at this extract from *The Lion Who Stole My Arm*. Circle the clues in the text that might explain how the characters are feeling and why. Use these clues to help you answer the questions on page 53.

Remember to use your literal and inference skills, as well as personal experience to think about the characters' feelings and actions in the story.

Chapter Two

Pedru woke up in hospital. Or rather, outside the hospital on the veranda at the back, because all the beds inside were full. Pedru's father, Issa, was sitting beside him, fanning away the flies with an old newspaper.

"How did I get here?" Pedru asked.

His father smiled. "I put you on my back and cycled like a crazy man."

It was 20 kilometres over dirt roads from the village to the clinic at Madune. Even for Pedru's father, the best hunter in the village, probably in all of Africa, this was quite a feat.

Issa put down the newspaper and placed his big hand on top of Pedru's head. "Now, my son," he asked gently, "tell me, how do you feel?"

Issa had always told Pedru never to answer any question without thinking first. So Pedru thought hard about his answer. He turned his head and looked to his right. Where his arm had been was a bandaged stump, like a white stick, ending just above where the elbow had been. For a moment, Pedru's head swam and he shut his eyes. But when he opened them again his arm was still gone. It hurt badly where the doctor had sewn up the wound the lion had left, but Pedru knew it would stop hurting in time. The other pain, however, would not go away so easily.

1. Do you think this story might be about courage and acceptance? Explain why you say this.

   _____

   _____

   _____

2. How do you think Pedru felt when he woke up and saw where he was? Why do you think this?

   _____

   _____

   _____

3. Why do you think Issa carried Pedru on his back and 'cycled like a crazy man'?

   _____

   _____

   _____

4. How do you think Pedru felt when he looked at his bandaged stump? Explain why you say this.

   _____

   _____

   _____

5. What do you think 'the other pain' might have been for Pedru that would not go away so easily? Why do you say this?

   _____

   _____

   _____

How did you do?

People

Look at the picture and read the poem. Then answer the questions on page 55.

People

Some people talk and talk
and never say a thing.
Some people look at you
and birds begin to sing.

Some people laugh and laugh
and yet you want to cry.
Some people touch your hand
and music fills the sky.

Charlotte Zolotow

1. What is this poem about? Explain in your own words.

_____

_____

2. List what 'some people' do in the poem.

_____

_____

3. '...and <u>never</u> say a thing.' Which word below has the **opposite** meaning to the word 'never' in the poem?

☐ once ☐ always ☐ not ever

4. From clues in the poem, do you think the author finds some people 'boring'? Why do you say this?

_____

_____

5. Does the author suggest that some people can make you feel happy when they gaze at you? How do you know this?

_____

_____

Now write your own question and answer. Tick the box to show which type of question it is.

☐ literal question ☐ inference question ☐ evaluation question

Your question: _____

Your answer: _____

_____

How did you do?

Famous Vikings

Look at the pictures and read the information below. Then answer the questions on page 57.

The Vikings loved to tell thrilling stories about brave heroes from the past. Some of these stories might not be true.

Ragnar Hairy-Breeches was a terrifying king who once raided Paris.

Erik the Red was a fearless warrior and adventurer who explored Greenland.

Erik the Red's daughter Freydis was a skilled sailor who fought in battles.

Harald Hardrada was a clever leader who once dug a tunnel into an enemy castle.

1. Explain in your own words what this information is about.

_____

_____

_____

Think about the different question types and underline the clues in the questions below to help you answer them.

2. Who was a skilled sailor and fought in battles?

_____

3. Who surprised his enemy within their castle walls? How do you know?

_____

_____

4. Were the Vikings heroes or villains? Explain why you think this.

_____

_____

_____

_____

Now write your own question and answer. Tick the box to show which type of question it is.

☐ literal question   ☐ inference question   ☐ evaluation question

Your question: _____

_____

Your answer: _____

_____

How did you do?

57

Stanley Bagshaw and the Twenty Two Ton Whale

The whale stared out at Ted for a moment,
Then let out a strange gurgling sound.
Edward, who understood whale-talk (a bit),
Listened carefully, then wrote it all down.

What did he say, Ted?
[said Stanley].

[Said Ted]
Well, from what I can hear,
He's just on his way to the Arctic.

[Said Stan]
Well it's not along here!!!

The Arctic is up near the North Pole.
He's really come way off his track.
This canal only goes to Huddersgate.
He'll have to turn round and go back.

He can't turn round here
[said Edward].
There isn't enough room to spare.

Stan thought for a bit, then said...

I know. That's it!

The boatyard.
There's lots of room there!

Use the extract on page 58 to help you answer the questions below.

1. Where did Ted say the whale was going?

    _____

2. Why did Ted listen carefully before he wrote everything down?

    _____

    _____

3. The whale 'let out a <u>strange</u> gurgling sound'. Tick the box that has a similar meaning and the box that has an opposite meaning to the word 'strange'.

    synonym (similar): ☐ odd   ☐ usual   ☐ noisy

    antonym (opposite): ☐ bizarre   ☐ friendly   ☐ normal

4. How do you think Stan and Ted felt when they saw the whale in the canal? Give your reasons for saying this.

    _____

    _____

Now write your own question and answer. Tick the box to show which type of question it is.

☐ literal question   ☐ inference question   ☐ evaluation question

Your question: _____

_____

Your answer: _____

_____

How did you do?

How to build a survival shelter

Look at the pictures and read the information about how to build a survival shelter. Then answer the questions on page 61. Think about the different question types.

Remember: always take someone with you and let an adult know where you are going

HOW TO BUILD A SURVIVAL SHELTER

Have fun making your own survival shelter in the woods

1. Choose what kind of shelter to make:

   Sloping A-frame shelter

   backbone

   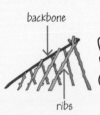

   ribs

   Use two shorter Y-shaped branches to hold up a long straight pole

   A tent-shaped shelter

   Find two trees fairly close together to rest a strong, straight branch between

   backbone — ribs

2. Add the ribs: collect straight branches and line them up along the length of your shelter.

   Then add some twiggy branches, weaving them between ribs to create a mesh.

3. Next add material to make it waterproof: work from bottom to top using whatever you can find on the ground.

   Bracken is great but wear gloves before picking it

   That's it! Now just crawl in and enjoy...

make sure there are no lumps or bumps on the ground

wildlife watch

www.wildlifewatch.org.uk

Illustration: Corinne Welch © copyright Royal Society of Wildlife Trusts 2015

1. List the materials you need to build a shelter in the woods.

_____

_____

2. Does the backbone of your shelter need to be sturdy when you are building a tent-shaped structure? How do you know this?

_____

_____

3. **a.** 'Then add some twiggy branches, weaving them between ribs to create a <u>mesh</u>.' What does the word 'mesh' mean here?
Tick the correct meaning.

☐ mess ☐ hole ☐ net

b. What do you think the 'mesh' is being used for here?

_____

4. Would you like to build your own survival shelter? Give your reasons.

_____

_____

Now write your own question and answer. Tick the box to show which type of question it is.

☐ literal question ☐ inference question ☐ evaluation question

Your question: _____

_____

Your answer: _____

_____

How did you do?

Mysterious Traveller

Read this extract from *Mysterious Traveller*. Then answer the questions on page 63. Think about the different question types.

The riders were slithering down into a low and rocky valley when Jin-Jin sensed a new danger. A danger far greater than the men following them. His clever nostrils read it in the air, and he roared a warning, digging his huge feet into the ground.

The rider leading him turned in his saddle and swore angrily. "On, Jin-Jin! On! *On!*" Then his face changed, because he saw what Jin-Jin had read on the wind. Behind them, the evening sky was now a boiling wall of sand and dust like a tidal wave.

A desert storm.

There was no time to find shelter. The storm hurtled into the valley and struck the travellers like an enormous fist, blinding them. The howling, whirling brown air blotted out the sun and the rocks and everything except itself.

The riders and their camels vanished into it.

1. Who is this passage about, what are they doing and where are they?

_____

2. Was Jin-Jin a rider or a camel? Explain how you know.

_____

_____

3. Do you think the riders were being chased? Why do you say this?

_____

_____

_____

4. Give an example of a metaphor and simile in the passage and explain why you think they are effective.

_____

_____

_____

Now write your own question and answer. Tick the box to show which type of question it is.

☐ literal question   ☐ inference question   ☐ evaluation question

Your question: _____

_____

Your answer: _____

_____

How did you do?

Awful Animals

Look at the pictures and read the information about the food web. Then answer the questions on page 65. Think about the different question types.

And now for three facts that will turn you into an instant zoologist. Oops, silly me. I bet you don't know what I'm talking about...

A **zoologist** is an animal scientist.

A **habitat** is the place an animal lives in.

THREE ANIMAL-TASTIC FACTS (don't turn the page until you've read them)...

1 *Every animal in the world has a habitat, where it finds food and shelter.*

OOER!

FOX = MEAT-EATING ANIMAL.

2 *Animals depend on one another...*

Meat-eating animals depend on plant-eating animals for food. And plant-eaters depend on meat-eaters. By eating weak and sick rabbits, foxes ensure that only the strongest bunnies get to mate, and this breeds strong, healthy rabbit families. And by keeping rabbit numbers down, the foxes stop the rabbits from guzzling all the grass and starving to death.

3 *Scientists describe the complicated feeding links between animals as a food web...*

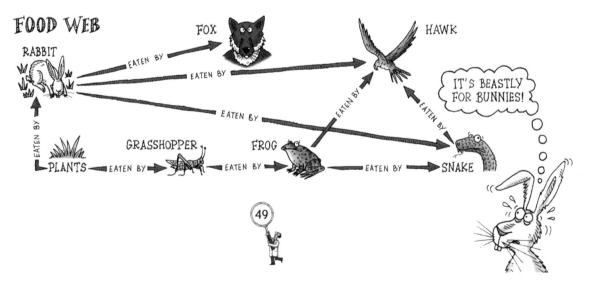

FOOD WEB

RABBIT — EATEN BY → FOX — EATEN BY → HAWK

PLANTS ← EATEN BY — GRASSHOPPER ← EATEN BY — FROG — EATEN BY → SNAKE

IT'S BEASTLY FOR BUNNIES!

49

1. List all the meat-eaters and plant-eaters in the food web.

   Meat-eaters: _____

   Plant-eaters: _____

2. Does the snake have the greatest choice of food in the food web? How do you know this?

   _____

   _____

3. Do you think the fox has any predators to worry about? Give your reason for saying this.

   _____

   _____

4. If you could be one of these creatures, which would you be and why?

   _____

   _____

Now write your own question and answer. Tick the box to show which type of question it is.

☐ literal question   ☐ inference question   ☐ evaluation question

Your question: _____
_____

Your answer: _____
_____

How did you do?

The Tragedy of King Richard III

Read this extract from a graphic version of one of Shakespeare's plays. Then answer the questions on pages 67 and 68.

In 1483, King Edward IV of England lay close to death. His son, the Prince of Wales, would inherit the crown even though he was still a child. The boy's uncle, hunchbacked Richard, Duke of Gloucester, had been made "Lord Protector" of the realm, and entrusted with the prince's care. But really Richard wanted the crown himself. And he was ready to use any means to get it, however foul…

Richard knew a king should have a well-born wife. He decided to court Anne, a royal widow. Since Richard himself had killed her husband and her father-in-law, Anne was disgusted when he came to woo her at the funeral. But the wily Richard talked so cleverly he won her round.

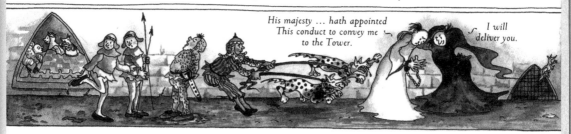

Richard also needed to be rid of his older brother, the popular Duke of Clarence. He persuaded the weakening King Edward to imprison him as a traitor in the terrible Tower of London. The unsuspecting Clarence loved Richard and trusted him to secure his release.

Think about the different question types as you answer the questions below. Then ask and answer your own literal, inference or evaluation question about the story.

1. What is this story about? Retell the main points in your own words.

   _____

   _____

   _____

2. Who is entrusted with the Prince's care?

   _____

3. Does Richard carry out more than one foul deed to help him secure the crown? How do you know this?

   _____

   _____

   _____

   _____

4. Why do you think Richard needs to be rid of his brother Clarence?

   _____

   _____

   _____

5. What do you think Anne means when she says to Richard, 'Out of my sight! Thou dost infect mine eyes.'

   _____

   _____

6. 'Richard knew a king should have a well-born wife. He decided to <u>court</u> Anne'. What do you think the word 'court' means here? Tick the correct meaning below.

☐ dance with ☐ challenge ☐ romance

7. What do you think becomes of Richard in the end? Why do you think this?

_____

_____

_____

8. What do you think this story tells us about wanting power for its own sake? Explain why you think this.

_____

_____

_____

_____

Now write your own question and answer. Tick the box to show which type of question it is.

☐ literal question   ☐ inference question   ☐ evaluation question

Your question: _____

_____

Your answer: _____

_____

How did you do?

Life on board ship: emigrant ships

Between 1800 and 1850 over three million men, women and children left the United Kingdom to begin new lives overseas. They travelled by ship to Canada, the USA, South Africa, Australia and New Zealand. Why did they go?

Thousands were driven out of Scotland because the landlords in the Highlands wanted to use the land for sheep farming. Thousands more were desperate to get away from Ireland because the potato crop had failed and people were dying of starvation. People emigrated from England and Wales because they were desperately poor and thought they would have a better life overseas.

The emigrants' lives depended on the captain and crew. It was their job to sail the ship skilfully, to make sure that the ship was kept clean, and to see that the emigrants had enough good food and water. Some voyages were disastrous. Between 1847 and 1853 over 50 emigrant ships were wrecked. Many emigrants fell ill on the journey. In 1852 there was a government enquiry into the ship *Ticonderoga* because 168 out its 814 passengers died on the journey to Australia.

Part of a letter written to her father by Mrs Phillips who emigrated to Australia in 1849.

WE LEFT PLYMOUTH ON 7TH FEBRUARY AND ARRIVED IN MELBOURNE ON 6TH JUNE. PHILIP WAS SICK A DAY OR TWO; JOHN AND ISAAC WERE QUITE AT HOME; MARY, ELIZA AND ELLEN WERE VERY WELL. WE HAD A VERY GOOD CAPTAIN BUT A VERY BAD DOCTOR. WE HAD SIX BIRTHS AND SEVEN DEATHS. WE HAD PLENTY OF FOOD, BUT THE LITTLE GIRLS' TEETH WERE NOT STRONG ENOUGH TO EAT THE BISCUITS. THE WATER CAME INTO A CALM AND WE LAY JUST IN ONE PLACE FOR THREE WEEKS. THE SAILORS CAUGHT FISH AND FOUR SHARKS. WE CAUGHT SEA BIRDS: THEY WERE VERY GOOD FOR EATING. WE HAD ONE GALE THEN WE GOT INTO A COLD CLIMATE.

Think about the different question types. Underline the clues in the questions to help you answer them.

1. What was the main reason for emigrants to make the hazardous journey abroad?

   _____

2. Did a large number of UK citizens emigrate in the first half of the nineteenth century? How do you know this?

   _____

   _____

3. Why do you think UK emigrants chose to live in Canada, the USA, South Africa, Australia and New Zealand?

   _____

   _____

   _____

   _____

4. Do you think life for UK emigrants might have been hard when they first arrived overseas? Why do you say this?

   _____

   _____

   _____

5. Why did emigrants' lives depend so much on their captain and his crew?

   _____

   _____

   _____

6. How long did it take Mrs Phillips and her family to sail to Australia? Explain how you know.

_____

_____

7. 'The water <u>came into a calm</u> and we lay just in one place for three weeks.' What do you think Mrs Phillips means when she says 'The water came into a calm'?

_____

_____

8. If you were an emigrant in the 1850s, which country would you choose to go to and why?

_____

_____

_____

Now write your own question and answer. Tick the box to show which type of question it is.

☐ literal question   ☐ inference question   ☐ evaluation question

Your question: _____

_____

Your answer: _____

_____

How did you do?

71

Progress chart

Tick (✔) Ollie when you have completed the chapter.

1 Retelling

2 Literal questioning

3 Prediction

7 Review

6 Evaluation

5 Clarification

4 Inference

Well done! You have now completed the Comprehension workbook for ages 9–10.